Thriving Blossoms

© AUTHOR

Sher Singh

(S S Chauhan)

Thriving Blossoms

Characters:

Falyn

- Female main character

Mitchel

- Male main character

Thriving Blossoms

Falyn has known Mitchel for two months now, and every day he drops by at her office to deliver a flower and keep her company. She had thought it wouldn't last long. But after a long day at work, she invites him to her place and quickly realizes the domesticity is something she craves all this time. So she offers him a place in her life.

Falyn gathers up her things, keeping all her necessities away in her handbag before pushing the chair in. 'Another tiring day.' She sighs mentally, giving her co-workers a wave, exchanging more pleasantries with them. With the bag caught under her arm, she hurries out of the building before she can be stopped by another colleague for more pointless conversations.

Thankfully, she manages to escape just fine, the elevator arrived soon after she called for it and she is well on her way out of her office. Working a 9 to 5 job is tiring, unnecessarily tiring. Between the terrible workload and the forced smiles thrown around, she is both physically and mentally exhausted. But still, she keeps up her smile, knowing her luck she might run into another colleague. It won't do to look upset here, others would think badly of her if they misunderstand.

She tries to look at the bright side, there's time to get home. Maybe she can cook something nice for herself. Though the thought of standing in the kitchen for any longer than 5 minutes is already irking her, she is very willing to give it a chance today. As she exits the building, there's a familiar figure standing there, like he had been waiting there for a long time.

His hands are hidden behind his back, and he fidgets around a lot. She can see, even from here, how his eyes light up with excitement after noticing her, and he rushes over to reveal a small flower in his hand.

"Good day at work I hope?" He asks. And she quickly realizes the dumb smile still plastered on her own face. So she allows herself to deflate a little, and he almost seems to do the same, "That bad?" He asks again, correcting the first question.

She accepts the flower, and promptly remembers that he has been keeping this up for two months at this point. "Thanks, I feel a little better now." Her lips twitch with a weak smile, "Just a lot of work to rush through. But I got it done at least. I can't handle another day of overtime work honestly."

He nods and walks with her, "You deserve the rest. There's no need to work that hard, you know?" That made her stop, and he does too, matching her pace by just a beat slower. "Mitchel, I know you're being sweet. But I want this promotion. To get that promotion, I have to work hard."

"But you're so tired. Look, you're burning

out. Or you will be, at this point. Just take it easy for some days. Please?" He gently takes her hand, hesitantly squeezing it and attempting to reassure her. It's easy for him to say, since he has a wonderful job with an equally wonderful pay.

Seeing that Falyn is not replying, he grips a little tighter around her hand, but is careful to not accidentally hurt her. It's simply a pressure that grounds her. "If you're tired, we can… I'll bring you to a nice restaurant, would you like that?" He tests his waters, smiling nervously at her, afraid that she would reject the invitation immediately.

Well, she wanted to cook. That was the plan earlier, but she is considering his offer. Not cooking sounds nice, but she doesn't want to piggy back off of him all the time, it doesn't feel right. Noticing her reluctance, he speaks again to interrupt her train of thoughts, "If you don't like that, we can do something else! I can drop by at your place? Cook for you?"

She raises a brow at him, "You can cook?" He gasps, in dramatic indignity, "Excuse me, I spent a lot of time perfecting my skills, just to cook for you. And now you question me?" He clutches at his heart, embarrassing himself, and her by association on the streets.

So Falyn quickly grabs at his arm, straightening him up, "Hush. Stop acting up. Fine fine. Prove to me you can cook then. Come on." She says to get him to stop. Immediately after, he stands upright and grins down at her in triumph, now dragging her along back to her place.

It's not the first time he dropped by, and it likely won't be the last either. Maybe she can get used to this, having someone pick her up at work, walk her home with a few jokes and laughs, then cook for her while she rests. It sounds so simple and domestic.

Before she even knows it, she is already standing in front of her door, and he's nudging her for the keys. Chuckling, she brings it out, unlocking the door and letting him rush for the kitchen. Seems like it was a good idea to stock up on ingredients yesterday. Hopefully there is enough of everything for him to make her a hearty meal, she desperately needs it right now.

After ditching her handbag on the couch, she sits at the table to watch him flit around the kitchen, reaching around the counters, the fridge and stove to begin preparing the food.

Takes him a while to get into the right pace, since he is still unfamiliar with where the utensils are.

Mitchel hums, she notices, when he is preoccupied. It's a soft tune that she can't exactly recognize. He busies himself in the kitchen, doing one thing at a time. It's clear that he's not well acquainted with the kitchen, but he's trying his best to make her a good dinner. And even if the food is looking just alright, it does smell delicious.

Took him almost 30 minutes of fumbling around for him to serve up two plates of food, and that confident grin he gives her made her smile too. Yeah, she can get used to this. Falyn waves at him to sit down next to her and they start eating. With the small vase of flowers in front of them, the blossoms at varying degrees of freshness, but remain as a testament of his perseverance. She decides that she quite likes this. So when their elbows touch, she gives him a playful smile and shifts just a tad closer.

Using only one hand to grip at the silverware, he places his hand over her free hand and smiles back at her. "I hope I proved myself with this meal." He chuckles.

Falyn laughs and nods, entwining her fingers with his, "Well… you can certainly do better. So keep practising, there's a lot more I want to try." She hints, rubbing her thumb over the back of his hand.

He catches on quick, eyes widening slightly, "So, I can drop by tomorrow? I can cook again." He offers eagerly, and she leans against his shoulder, "Sounds great, coming home to a warm meal. Sounds perfect."

****